America's Founders

Researching American History

introduced and edited by
Pat Perrin

The Philadelphia State House, also known as Independence Hall, where the Federal Convention met during the summer of 1787. (Courtesy of the Library of Congress)

Discovery Enterprises, Ltd.
Carlisle, Massachusetts

First Edition © Discovery Enterprises, Ltd., Carlisle, MA 2003

ISBN: 1 57960 097-2

Library of Congress Catalog Card Number 2003101147

10 9 8 7 6 5 4 3 2 1

Printed in the United States of America

Subject Reference Guide:

Title: *America's Founders*
Series*: Researching American History*
introduced and edited by Pat Perrin

Credits:

Cover art: Continental Congress, May 1775. In the chair *(far left)* sits John Hancock, President of the Congress. Standing in the middle of the room is John Adams about to propose Colonel Washington for commander in chief of the Continental armies. As Washington *(far right)* realizes that his name is before the Congress, he rises and slips out of the room so that the delegates can discuss him freely. From *Pictorial History of American Presidents,* by John and Alice Durant, New York: A. S. Barnes and Company, 1955, p. 8.

Mediasource illustrations: pp. 5, 7, 14, 19, 24, 28, 30, 35, and 42.

All other illustrations credited where they appear in the text.

Contents

About the Series

Researching American History is a series of books which introduces various topics and periods in our nation's history through the study of primary source documents.

Reading the Historical Documents

On the following pages you'll find words written by people during or soon after the time of the events. This is firsthand information about what life was like back then. Illustrations are also created to record history. These historical documents are called **primary source materials**.

At first, some things written in earlier times may seem difficult to understand. Language changes over the years, and the objects and activities described might be unfamiliar. Also, spellings were sometimes different. Below is a model which describes how we help with these challenges.

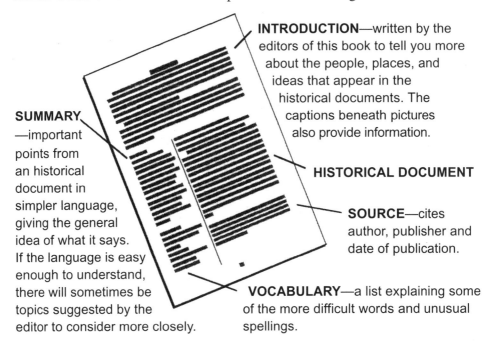

INTRODUCTION—written by the editors of this book to tell you more about the people, places, and ideas that appear in the historical documents. The captions beneath pictures also provide information.

SUMMARY —important points from an historical document in simpler language, giving the general idea of what it says. If the language is easy enough to understand, there will sometimes be topics suggested by the editor to consider more closely.

HISTORICAL DOCUMENT

SOURCE—cites author, publisher and date of publication.

VOCABULARY—a list explaining some of the more difficult words and unusual spellings.

In these historical documents, you may see three periods (…) called an ellipsis. It means that the editor has left out some words or sentences. You may see some words in brackets, such as [and]. These are words the editor has added to make the meaning clearer. When you use a document in a paper you're writing, you should include any ellipses and brackets it contains, just as you see them here. Be sure to give complete information about the author, title, and publisher of anything that was written by someone other than you.

Drafting the Declaration of Independence

Introduction: America's Founders
by Pat Perrin

This book is about people who created the United States of America. At first, they were British citizens. Starting in the early 1600s, England founded 13 colonies along the east coast of the New World. (To found something means to establish it—to be its original builder or creator.) In the late 1700s, some people who lived in these colonies began to think of their land as a separate country.

Many men worked together to change the English colonies into a new American nation. Although women could not hold power at that time, some of the men took their opinions into account. On the following pages you'll find words that were spoken or written by many of the most important of our nation's founders.

The nation's beginnings are covered in greater detail in other books from Discovery Enterprises. In the *Researching American History* series, see *The Revolutionary War, The Declaration of Independence,* and *The Constitution and the Bill of Rights.* In the *Perspectives on History* series, see *The Shot Heard 'Round the World, The French and Indian War, The Declaration of Independence,* and *The Constitution and the Bill of Rights.*

To help you connect these events and the individuals who lived through them, this book includes several lists of important dates. On the following page is a brief overview of what happened.

Dates and Events—A New Nation

1760–70s American colonists become increasingly unhappy with British policies, especially taxes

1774   The First Continental Congress (the first legislature for the13 colonies) meets in Philadelphia

1775   Colonial militias battle with British troops; the Second Continental Congress chooses George Washington to lead the Colonial Army

1776   Congress adopts the Declaration of Independence

1776–83 The Revolutionary War

1781   Congress ratifies (officially approves) the Articles of Confederation, creating the first United States government

1787   Delegates to a Federal Convention at Philadelphia declare themselves a Constitutional Convention; they write a new Constitution

1787-88 The states all ratify the Constitution

1789   George Washington elected our first president; John Adams, vice president; Alexander Hamilton becomes secretary of the treasury; Thomas Jefferson becomes secretary of state

1791   The Bill of Rights is adopted by Congress

1792   Washington reelected for a second term

1797   John Adams elected president; Thomas Jefferson, vice president

1801   Thomas Jefferson elected president, Aaron Burr, vice president; James Madison becomes secretary of state.

1804   Jefferson reelected president

1804   Alexander Hamilton killed in a duel with Aaron Burr

1809   James Madison elected president, reelected in 1812

Political Parties

When the nation was founded, there were no political parties. It was thought that good leaders could be elected without parties. George Washington was opposed to the idea of parties. At first, Thomas Jefferson also refused to identify himself as a member of any party. But some politicians wanted a strong central government with special favors for industry, landowners, and merchants. Alexander Hamilton became the leader of that group—the Federalists. Other politicians wanted to limit central power and give more to the states and individuals. Eventually Thomas Jefferson became the leader of that group—the Republicans.

John Adams

Adams (1735-1826) was born in Massachusetts, where his father was a farmer and a church deacon. Educated for college, he graduated from Harvard, taught grammar school, and studied law. He married a minister's daughter, Abigail Smith, who was to become his best friend and advisor during his political career.

Early in the move toward independence, Adams was an active critic of British colonial policies. He especially objected to the Stamp Act, which taxed the colonies without colonists' approval. However, Adams believed in justice for all, so he helped defend British soldiers accused of murder in the "Boston Massacre."

Adams was outspoken but could also be good-humored and down to earth. He didn't care about the current fashions, and was sometimes referred to as "his rotundity" when he presided over the Senate. In the election for our first president, George Washington received the most votes; Adams received the second highest number. Under the rules of the time, that made him the vice president. When political parties formed, Adams became one of the leading Federalists.

Adams' first son, John Quincy, would become the sixth president in 1825. Like Thomas Jefferson, John Adams died 50 years to the day after the formal Declaration of Independence.

Dates and Events—John Adams

1755	Graduates from Harvard; teaches grammar school and studies law; admitted to the Boston Bar in 1758
1763	Contributes stories to several different newspapers, sometimes carrying on a discussion with himself
1764	Marries Abigail Smith
1765	Begins to express disapproval of the British—especially their failure to recognize the equality of men and the rights of the colonists
1768	Defends John Hancock against charges of smuggling.
1770	Believing in the importance of fair trials, defends the British soldiers accused of murder in the "Boston Massacre"
1774	Massachusetts delegate to the First Continental Congress
1775	Begins to urge independence from England; publishes letters and essays arguing for colonies' rights to govern themselves; nominates George Washington to be commander in chief of the new Colonial Army
1776	Appointed to the committee to draft a Declaration of Independence; defends the document in Congress; is one of 56 signers of the Declaration
1776–78	Serves on several congressional committees, including ones to create a navy and to review foreign affairs
1778	Serves with Benjamin Franklin as a joint commissioner to France
1779	Returns home, helps draft the Massachusetts state constitution; again sent to Europe. Two sons accompany him, and in 1784 his wife and daughter join him there.
1785	Becomes the first U.S. minister to England
1787	While in England, publishes his "Defence of the Constitutions of Government of the United States of America" suggesting that only certain kind of people—"the rich, the well-born and the able"—should serve in the upper chamber of the government. This attitude offended some in America.
1788	Returns to America
1789	Elected first vice president
1797	Elected second president

In the Words of John Adams

1776—A More Equal Liberty

The dons, the bashaws, the grandees, the patricians, the sachems, the nabobs, call them by what names you please, sigh and groan and fret, and sometimes stamp and foam and curse, but all in vain. The decree is gone forth, and it cannot be recalled, that a more equal liberty than has prevailed in other parts of the earth must be established in America.

Source: John Adams, letter to Patrick Henry, June 3, 1776, found in "Founding Fathers Quotes" at http://www.foundingfathers.info/quotes/archive/1.html

Summary:

Those who hold power may object, but the order has been given and can't be taken back. A more equal freedom than has existed anywhere else must be set up in America.

Vocabulary:

dons, bashaws, grandees, patricians, sachems, nabobs = the rich and powerful
established = legally recognized; supported
prevailed = been in force

1776—What's a Government For?

Upon this point all speculative politicians will agree, that the happiness of society is the end of government, as all divines and moral philosophers will agree that the happiness of the individual is the end of man. From this principle it will follow that the form of government which communicates ease, comfort, security, or, in one word, happiness, to the greatest numbers of persons, and in the greatest degree, is the best.

Source: John Adams, *Thoughts on Government,* 1776, found in "Founding Fathers Quotes" at http://www.foundingfathers.info/quotes/archive/1.html

Consider this:

Adams says that the government's reason for being is the happiness of society. In what ways do you think our government meets or fails to meet this standard?

Vocabulary:

divines = those who foresee the future
end = aim; intention
moral philosophers = those who study the principles of right and wrong behavior
speculative = thinking

Consider this:
What subjects does John Adams believe are most important for people to study?

Vocabulary:
philosophy = the study of basic ideas such as truth, freedom, reality
porcelain = fine ceramics
statuary = sculpture

1780—Working for a Better Future

I must study politics and war that my sons may have liberty to study mathematics and philosophy. My sons ought to study mathematics and philosophy, geography, natural history and naval architecture, navigation, commerce and agriculture, in order to give their children a right to study painting, poetry, music, architecture, statuary, tapestry, and porcelain.

Source: John Adams, letter to Abigail Adams, May 12, 1780, in "Adams Quotations," found at http://www.masshist.org/apquotes.html

Consider this:
Since Adams obviously would rather have been at home—why do you suppose he was in Philadelphia?

Vocabulary:
affected = not natural; meant to impress others
constrained = self-conscious, not behaving naturally
drawing rooms = formal living rooms
levees = court receptions
proclamations = public announcements
relinquish = give up

1796—"I Hate Speeches"

Philadelphia, 1 March, 1796

I hate to live in Philadelphia in summer, and I hate still more to relinquish my farm. I hate speeches, messages, addresses and answers, proclamations, and such affected, studied, constrained things. I hate levees and drawing rooms. I hate to speak to a thousand people to whom I have nothing to say. Yet all this I can do.

Source: John Adams Letter to Abigail Adams, *Letters of John Adams,* Vol. II, Boston: Charles C Little and James Brown, XXXX, p. 207.

1797—Looking Back at the Constitution, John Adams' Inaugural Address

Employed in the service of my country abroad during the whole course of these transactions, I first saw the Constitution of the United States in a foreign country.... I read it with great satisfaction, as the result of good heads prompted by good hearts, as an experiment better adapted to the genius, character, situation, and relations of this nation and country than any which had ever been proposed or suggested. In its general principles and great outlines it was conformable to such a system of government as I had ever most esteemed, and in some States, my own native State in particular, had contributed to establish....

. . . .

What other form of government, indeed, can so well deserve our esteem and love?

Source: John Adams, Inaugural Address, Philadelphia, Saturday, March 4, 1797, *The Avalon Project at Yale Law School,* found at http://www.yale.edu/lawweb/avalon/presiden/inaug/adams.html

Summary:

I was overseas when the Constitution was written. When I saw it, I was very pleased at the job those good minds, urged by good hearts, had done. It was better for our nation than anything suggested before. In general, it fit the kind of government that I had most hoped for. Some states, my own in particular, had worked to set up such a system....

What other kind of government could deserve our praise and love?

Vocabulary:

conformable = similar to; consistent with

esteemed = highly valued

transactions = dealings

1800—A Prayer on First Occupying the White House

Presidents house, Washington City
Nov. 2. 1800

Before I end my Letter I pray Heaven to bestow the best of Blessings on this House and all that shall hereafter inhabit it. May none but honest and wise Men ever rule under this roof....

Source: John Adams letter to Abigail Adams, 2 November 1800, *Letters of John Adams,* Vol. II, Boston: Charles C. Little and James Brown, 1841, p. 267.

Commentary:

As president, Adams was the first to live in the executive mansion in the new capital city of Washing-ton, D.C.

Franklin Delano Roosevelt —our 32nd president—had Adams' prayer for the executive mansion placed above the mantel in the State Dining Room of the White House.

Aaron Burr

Aaron Burr was charming, witty, and intelligent. In the 1801 presidential election, Burr got just as many votes as Thomas Jefferson did. According to the rules of the time, whoever got the most votes became president and whoever came in second became vice president. So Congress had to choose the president—and they chose Jefferson.

Burr and Alexander Hamilton were longtime political enemies. In 1804 their disagreements got so bad that Burr challenged Hamilton to a duel. When they fought, Burr shot Hamilton, who died of his wound. After that, Burr never again held a position of power in the United States.

Consider this:

What do you think of Burr's advice?

How do you think these ideas would work for a politician?

Burr's Advice

"Never do today what you can put off till to-morrow. Delay may give clearer light as to what is best to be done."

Source: Arron Burr, found at http://www.quoteworld.org/browse.

The rule of my life is to make business a pleasure, and pleasure my business.

Source: Arron Burr letter, found at http://www.giga-usa.com/gigaweb1/quotes2/quautburraaronx001.htm

John Dickinson, (1732–1808), studied law in London, and became a well-known trial lawyer in Philadelphia. He worked with Thomas Jefferson to write the 1775 "Declaration of the Causes for Taking Up Arms." He also worked with John Jay to get the "Olive Branch" petition passed. Dickinson held political positions in both Delaware and Pennsylvania, and was a member of the Continental Congress, and the Constitutional Convention.

John Dickinson

In the 1760s, John Dickinson objected to many British policies, but he believed that the problems could be worked out peacefully. When the colonies actually declared independence, Dickinson refused to sign the Declaration. However, he helped draft the Articles of Confederation and represented Delaware at the Constitutional Convention. He helped design a two-house form of representation to satisfy both the smallest and largest states. Because he was ill, a friend signed Dickinson's name to the new Constitution, then Dickinson worked hard to get the Constitution ratified.

Date—Letters From A Farmer

Here then, my dear country men ROUSE yourselves, and behold the ruin hanging over your heads. If you ONCE admit, that Great-Britain may lay duties upon her [exports] to us, for the purpose of levying money on us only, she then will have nothing to do, but to lay those duties on the articles which she prohibits us to manufacture—and … American liberty is finished.

Source: John Dickinson, "Letters From a Farmer II," in *From Revolution to Reconstruction*—an HTML project, found at http://odur.let.rug.nl/~usa/D/1751-1775/townshend/dickII.htm

Commentary:
In 1768, Dickinson's "Letters from a Farmer in Pennsylvania to the Inhabitants of the British Colonies" were widely read. Here, he objects to high taxes on British products that the colonists weren't allowed to make for themselves.

Vocabulary:
levying = collecting
rouse = wake up; stir

Benjamin Franklin

Franklin (1706-1790) led a long and busy life—too full to describe in much detail here. Taken out of grammar school to help his father make candles and soap, he had very little formal education. But by age 10, Franklin loved to read, and he borrowed books wherever he could. At age 16, Franklin started turning in his own essays to his half-brother's newspaper—by slipping them under the door at night. According to the essays, they were written by widow named Silence Dogood. Readers loved them, but Franklin's brother was furious when he found out who wrote them.

Young Franklin ran away to New York City, but couldn't find work. But he didn't give up easily. He walked across New Jersey to Philadelphia, where he got a job in a print shop. Later he was promised funds to open his own printing business. So he borrowed money and traveled to London, England to buy equipment. When the money didn't come through, he worked in London to earn his passage home. All of that happened by the time he was 20.

Franklin seemed to think about absolutely everything around him. He studied French, Italian, Spanish, and Latin. His many inventions include a new type of stove, and his experiments with electricity brought him fame. He founded the Philadelphia Fire Company, library, city police, a hospital, an Academy that became the University of Pennsylvania, and the American Philosophical Society.

He traveled to England and France many times, representing several different colonies or states. He served as Postmaster General, and served the public in many ways. When the Constitution was written, Franklin was 82.

Dates and Events—Benjamin Franklin

1718	Apprenticed to his half-brother, James, to learn printing trade
1722	The Silence Dogood essays published in brother's newspaper
1723	Runs away, gets a job in a Philadelphia print shop
1724	Goes to London to buy printing equipment
1727-29	Owner and editor of the "Pennsylvania Gazette"
1730	Marries Deborah Read
1732	Publishes the first "Poor Richard's Almanac" under the name "Richard Saunders"; the Almanac—full of Franklin's own witty sayings—continues for 25 years.
1737	Elected to the Pennsylvania Assembly
1746	Forms a military company; begins electrical experiments
1749	Appointed a Commissioner to trade with the Indians
1752	Experiments with a kite and discovers that lightning is electrical
1753	Receives international honors, university degrees from Yale and Harvard; appointed joint Postmaster-General
1754	Commissioner from Pennsylvania to the Colonial Congress; proposes a plan for the union of the colonies
1755	Carries through a bill establishing a voluntary militia; appointed Colonel, fights in the French and Indian War
1762	In London, receives a degree from Oxford
1765	Tries to prevent the passage of the Stamp Act
1775	Delegate to the Second Continental Congress
1776	On the committee to draft a declaration of independence
1782-83	In Paris, signs the preliminary articles of peace and the peace treaty ending the Revolutionary War
1785	Chosen President of Pennsylvania
1787	Delegate to the Federal convention for framing a new Constitution
1788	Retires from public life

In the Words of Benjamin Franklin

Commentary:

In 1726, Franklin had earned enough money to pay his way home after he was stranded in London (see page 14). On board the ship, he apparently gave some thought to how he would spend his life. In his journal, he wrote down some rules for how he would behave. In his autobiography, he commented that he had kept his rules pretty faithfully. That part of the journal is missing, but a few of the rules survived.

Consider this:

What do you think of Franklin's rules for life?

What rules would you write down for yourself?

Vocabulary:

apt = likely

frugal = thrifty; avoiding expense

henceforth = from now on

incongruity = something that doesn't fit with others; inconsistency

rational =using good sense; able to think clearly

1726—A Plan for Future Conduct

Those who write of the art of poetry teach us that if we would write what may be worth the reading, we ought always, before we begin, to form a regular plan and design of our piece: otherwise, we shall be in danger of incongruity. I am apt to think it is the same as to life. I have never fixed a regular design in life; by which means it has been a confused variety of different scenes. I am now entering upon a new one: let me, therefore, make some resolutions, and form some scheme of action, that henceforth I may live in all respects like a rational creature.

1. It is necessary for me to be extremely frugal for some time, till I have paid what I owe.

2. To endeavour to speak truth in every instance; to give nobody expectations that are not likely to be answered, but aim at sincerity in every word and action—the most amiable excellence in a rational being.

3. To apply myself industriously to whatever business I take in hand, and not divert my mind from my business by any foolish project of growing suddenly rich; for industry and patience are the surest means of plenty.

4. I resolve to speak ill of no man whatever, not even in a matter of truth; but rather by some means excuse the faults I hear charged upon others, and upon proper occasions speak all the good I know of every body.

Source: Benjamin Franklin, *Autobiographical Writings,* Carl Van Doren, ed., New York: The Viking Press, 1945, p. 25.

This cartoon, probably drawn by Benjamin Franklin, appeared in the Pennsylvania Gazette *on May 9, 1754. It is thought to be the first American political cartoon. According to a belief of that time, a snake could be broken into pieces and then rejoined, and live. Franklin was urging the colonies to unite against the French—and warning them that they would perish if they didn't get together.*

1775

They that can give up essential liberty to obtain a little temporary safety deserve neither liberty nor safety.

Source: Benjamin Franklin, in the *Historical Review of Pennsylvania,* from John Bartlett, *Familiar Quotations,* 10th ed., 1919.

1783

There never was a good war or a bad peace.

Source: Benjamin Franklin, Letter, July 27, 1783, to the botanist Sir Joseph Banks. Complete Works, vol. 8, ed. John Bigelow (1887-1888). Franklin also used the same words in a letter of Sept. 11, 1783, to New England revolutionary Josiah Quincy. From *The Columbia World of Quotations,* Columbia University Press, 1996.

Commentary:
Franklin was known for his short and insightful comments, and they appear in many collections of quotations. These were found on Bartleby.com

Vocabulary:
essential = basic; necessary

Although he often planned to retire, Franklin was called into public service again and again. He was first elected clerk of the Pennsylvania Assembly in 1736. In 1787, he was in his third term as President of that state.

1787—Public Service

Philadelphia, November 4, 1787

… I have now been upwards of fifty years employed in public offices. When I informed your good friend Dr. Cooper that I was ordered to France, being then seventy years old, and observed that the public, having as it were eaten my flesh, seemed now resolved to pick my bones, he replied that he approved their taste, for that the nearer the bone the sweeter the meat.

Source: Benjamin Franklin, letter to his sister, *Autobiographical Writings,* Carl Van Doren, ed., New York: The Viking Press, 1945, p. 686.

Commentary:

By 1788, Franklin was troubled with various illnesses, and finally retired from public service. He had seen his country grow from separate colonies into an independent nation that developed a new form of government.

1788—The Constitution

Philadelphia, June 8, 1788

… Eight States have now agreed to the proposed new Constitution; there remain five who have not yet discussed it; their appointed times of meeting not being yet arrived. Two are to meet this month, the rest later. One more agreeing, it will be carried into execution. Probably some will not agree at present, but time may bring them in; so that we have little doubt of its becoming general, perhaps with some corrections. As to your friend's taking a share in the management of it, his age and infirmities render him unfit for the business, as the business would be for him.… General Washington is the man that all our eyes are fixed on for *President,* and what little influence I may have is devoted to him. I am, etc.

Source: Benjamin Franklin, letter to a friend, *Autobiographical Writings,* Carl Van Doren, ed., New York: The Viking Press, 1945, p 687.

Alexander Hamilton

Hamilton was born in the West Indies, sometime between 1755 and 1757. He died in 1804, after being shot in a duel with Aaron Burr. Hamilton's parents weren't legally married, and his father left his mother in 1765. At age 11, Hamilton went to work as a bookkeeper, and did such a good job that he was soon promoted to office manager. Recognizing the boy's intelligence, a minister and a businessman paid for his education in America. He was an outstanding student at a preparatory school in New Jersey and at what is now Columbia University.

In the Revolutionary War, Hamilton was an aide to General George Washington, the commander of the American forces. After the war, he began to be successful in American politics. At the Constitutional Convention, he argued for a strong central government. He helped shape the new constitution, and signed it as an individual, even though he didn't have the support of his state of New York.

Hamilton wrote many essays in defense of the new Constitution and the government it shaped. Along with James Madison and John Jay, he wrote essays that were later called *The Federalist Papers*. Those essays helped get the Constitution ratified by the states.

Under the new Constitution, George Washington became America's first president. He made Alexander Hamilton his first secretary of treasury. The boy who started work as a bookkeeper had grown into a man who was in charge of the finances of a nation.

Hamilton developed strong opinions about what the United States government should be like. Over the years, he made many enemies, including Aaron Burr. When the first political parties formed, he led the Federalists—those in favor of a strong central government. The Federalists were opposed by the Republicans, led by Thomas Jefferson—those who wanted more power for the states and less for the federal government.

Dates and Events—Alexander Hamilton

1773	Enters King's College (later Columbia University), but his studies are cut short by early acts of colonial revolt against Great Britain
1774–75	Writes three anonymous pamphlets defending actions of the Continental Congress
1776–77	Captain in the provincial artillery; becomes lieutenant colonel as Washington's aide.
1780	Marries Elizabeth Schuyler, from one of New York's most important families
1781	In command of a battalion; at Yorktown, leads an assault on the British
1782	Studies law, admitted to law practice; elected a New York delegate to the Continental Congress, he works for a strong central government
1783	Practices law in New York City; defends unpopular Loyalists who remained faithful to the British during the Revolution
1786	Delegate to the Federal convention, drafts the address to the states from which emerged the Constitutional Convention
1787	Delegate to the Constitutional Convention; major author of the *Federalist Papers*
1789–95	First secretary of the Treasury of the United States
1804	Killed in duel with Aaron Burr

In the Words of Alexander Hamilton

1769—Hamilton at 14

Dear Edward

… To confess my weakness, Ned, my Ambition is prevalent. That I contemn the grov'ling condition of a Clerk or the like, to which my Fortune &c condemns me and would willingly risk my life though not my Character to exalt my station, I'm confident, Ned that my Youth excludes me from any hopes of immediate Perferment, nor do I desire it but I mean to prepare the way for futurity, I'm no Philosopher you see and may be justly said to Build Castles in the Air, my Folly makes me ashamed and beg youll conceal it, yet Neddy we have seen such schemes successful when the Projector is Constant. I shall Conclude saying I wish there was a war.

I am
dr Edward
yours
Alex Hamilton

Source: Alexander Hamilton, Letter to Edward Stevens, found at http://xroads. virginia.edu/~CAP/ham/LTR I 769.htm They note that the letter is reprinted from Broadus Mitchell, *Heritage from Hamilton*, 1957.

Summary:

To confess my weakness, Ned, my ambition is strong. I feel contempt for the lowly life of a Clerk or anything like that, to which fate condemns me. I would willingly risk my life, though not my character, to raise my station. I'm sure, Ned, that my youth prevents quick advancement. I don't even want that, but I'm preparing for the future. I'm no great thinker, you see, and I build castles in the air. My foolishness makes me ashamed and I beg you'll hide it. Yet we have seen such schemes work when the schemer doesn't give up. I'll end saying I wish there was a war.

Vocabulary:

contemn = view with
    contempt
exalt = raise in rank
grov'ling = groveling;
    crawling in fear or to
    show false respect
perferment = preference;
    being chosen over
    another
prevalent = prevailing;
    strong; effective

Summary:
I've tried, fellow-citizens, to show you the importance of the Union to your safety and happiness.

According to plan, the next point is the "inadequacy of the Articles of Confederation to preserve the Union." In general, most seem to agree that there are problems in our national system and that some-thing must be done to save us from approaching anarchy.

Commentary:
In 1787-88, a series of political essays signed "Publius" appeared in New York newspapers. Alexander Hamilton wrote most of the essays; James Madison and John Jay wrote the others. Called *The Federalist Papers,* they argue for the ratification of the new constitution.

Vocabulary:
anarchy = a lack of
   government or controls
endeavored = tried to
   achieve something
impending = about to
   happen

1777-78—The Federalist Papers

To the People of the State of New York.

… I have endeavored, my fellow-citizens, to place before you, in a clear and convincing light, the importance of Union to your political safety and happiness.…

In pursuance of the plan which I have laid down for the discussion of the subject, the point next in order to be examined is the "insufficiency of the present Confederation to the preservation of the Union." … [Citizens] in general appear to harmonize in this sentiment, at least, that there are material imperfections in our national system, and that something is necessary to be done to rescue us from impend-ing anarchy.…

PUBLIUS.

Source: Alexander Hamilton, Federalist No. 15, "The Insufficiency of the Present Confederation to Preserve the Union," originally in the *Independent Journal,* found at http://www.foundingfathers.info/federalistpapers/fed15.htm

1788—The Two Aims of Government

There are two objects in forming systems of government—Safety for the people, and energy in the administration. When these objects are united, the certain tendency of the system will be to the public welfare. If the latter object be neglected, the people's security will be as certainly sacrificed, as by disregarding the former. Good constitutions are formed upon a comparison of the liberty of the individual with the strength of government: If the tone of either be too high, the other will be weakened too much…. Through the opposition and mutual controul of [the house of representatives and the senate], the government will reach, in its regular operations, the perfect balance between liberty and power.

Source: Alexander Hamilton, statement at the New York Ratifying Convention, June 25, 1788, from *The Papers of Alexander Hamilton,* Harold C. Syrett, ed. 26 vols. New York and London: Columbia University Press, 1961--79, 5:81. Found on "The Founders' Constitution" web site, The University of Chicago Press, at http://press-pubs.uchicago.edu/founders/documents/v1ch12s24.html

Summary:

There are two reasons for forming systems of government—safety for the people, and power for the government. When these aims work together, the system will work for the public good. If the second one is neglected, then the people's safety will be lost as surely as if the first one is ignored. Good constitutions balance individual liberty with strong government. If either is set too high, the other will be weakened too much. When the two legislative houses are in opposition and have equal control, the government will reach, naturally, the perfect balance between liberty and power.

Vocabulary:

controul = control
objects = aims; purposes
tendency = likely behavior
tone = quality; general
    nature

John Hancock

Hancock (1737-1793) was born in Massachusetts. As a boy, he lived with his uncle, who was a wealthy merchant. With training from his uncle and a degree from Harvard, John Hancock became a successful businessman. When British taxes got higher and higher, that was hard on his business. So Hancock became active in politics. As the leader of the Second Continental Congress, he was the first to sign the Declaration of Independence—with his famous large signature.

After the Declaration, Hancock hoped to become commander-in-chief of the Continental Army. When George Washington was selected instead, he went back to Massachusetts politics, becoming that state's first governor. In 1788, he had some doubts about the new Constitution because of the powers it gave the central government. Nevertheless, he gave it his approval, and others followed his lead.

Dates and Events—John Hancock

1754   Graduates from Harvard; enters his uncle's mercantile (commercial trading) house in Boston

1765   Selectman of Boston (a member of the governing board elected in most New England towns)

1769–74   Member of the Massachusetts General Court

1770   Chairman of the Boston town committee formed to demand the removal of British troops from the city

1774–75   President of the first and second Massachusetts provincial congresses; a leader of the Massachusetts Patriots; forced to flee Lexington for Philadelphia when British troops come looking for him

1775–80   Member of the Continental Congress; its president from May 1775 to October 1777

1776   Signs the Declaration of Independence

1780   Elected governor of Massachusetts

1785-86   Serves in the Congress under the Articles of Confederation, then returns to the Massachusetts governorship

1788   Presides over the Massachusetts Convention that ratifies the Federal Constitution

John Hancock's signature was the first and largest on the Declaration of Independence.

In the Words of John Hancock

Summary:

We cannot see what will happen because of our actions. But we still have a duty to ourselves and our descendents to do the best we can in our public decisions.… Congress has decided we must dissolve all connections between Great Britain and the American Colonies, and to declare them free and independent states —as you will see this by the enclosed Declaration. … I request you have it announced in your colony however you think best.

Commentary:

The Declaration had been passed and printed. As president of the Continental Congress, Hancock wrote to the Governor of Rhode Island.

Vocabulary:

consequences = results
counsels = discussions
   with others
posterity = future
   generations
proclaimed = announced
   publicly
transmit = pass along

1776—Spreading the Word

Philadelphia
July 6th, 1776.

Sir,

Altho it is not possible to foresee the Consequences of human Actions, yet it is nonetheless a Duty we owe ourselves and Posterity in all our public Counsels, to decide in the best Manner we are able, and to trust the load to that Being who controls both Causes and Events, so as to bring about his own Determination.

…The Congress have judged it necessary to dissolve all Connection between Great Britain and the American Colonies, and to declare them free and independent States; as you will perceive by the enclosed Declaration, which I am directed to transmit to you, and to request you will have it proclaimed in your Colony, in the Way you shall think most proper.

The Services in the Northern Department requiring a Number of Ship Carpenters to build Vessels for the Defense of the Lakes, I am directed by Congress to request you will order fifty to be immediately engaged, and sail to General Schuyler at Albany for that Purpose. You will naturally endeavour to engage them on the best Terms. I enclose to you the Terms on which the Marine Committee have engaged a Number for the same Business. But should you not be able to procure them at the same Rate, it is the Desire of Congress, you should exceed it, rather than the Carpenters should not be sent.

I have the Honour to be, Sir, your most h[um]ble Ser[vant],
John Hancock, President

Source: John Hancock letter to Governor Nicholas Cooke of Rhode Island, from the Lilly Library U.S. History mss., found at http://www.indiana.edu/~liblilly/history/hancocktext.html

Summary:
The military in the north needs carpenters to build ships for the defense of the Great Lakes. Congress directs me to request that you order 50 carpenters to be hired right away, and to send them to Albany. You will naturally try to get the best deal with them. Enclosed is a copy of the terms the Marine Committee has paid carpenters before. But if you can't get them for that rate, pay them more rather than not sending them.

Commentary:
In his letter that he sent with a copy of the Declaration of Independence, Hancock began preparations to defend the new country —which was already at war.

Vocabulary:
endeavour = endeavor; make an effort
engage = hire
procure = obtain
terms = the conditions of an agreement

Patrick Henry (1736-99) was a Virginian. He was mostly self-educated, but became a well-known lawyer. He was most famous for his stirring public speeches. Henry was a member of the House of Burgesses and the Continental Congress. He was governor of Virginia 1776-1779, where he led a fight for religious freedom.

Patrick Henry

Henry felt very strongly that the colonies should declare their independence from England. In 1775, he made his famous speech to the Virginia Assembly, saying "I know not what course others may take; but as for me, give me liberty or give me death."

He believed just as strongly that the states should hold power, rather than a central government. He was appointed a Virginia Delegate to the Constitutional convention, but refused to attend. He considered the new system of government "a loss of liberty."

After the new Constitution had been ratified by the states, Patrick Henry agreed to accept it. However, he planned to amend it as soon as possible—and he did. Henry helped push through the Bill of Rights. Although he was an anti-federalist at the convention, he later joined the Federalist party.

Commentary:

Once the Constitution had been ratified, a number of founders set about correcting it. That resulted in the passage of the first ten amendments—called Bill of Rights—in 1791.

1788—Accepting the Constitution

I will be a peaceable citizen . . . My head, my hand, and my heart shall be at liberty to retrieve the loss of liberty, and remove the defects of that system in a constitutional way.

Source: Patrick Henry, found in Richard Hofstadter, William Miller, and Daniel Aaron, *The United States: History of a Republic,* Englewood Cliffs, New Jersey: Prentice-Hall, 1962, p. 134.

John Jay (1745-1829) was born in New York City. He graduated from what is now Columbia University, and became a lawyer. He was appointed chief justice of New York, then became president of the Continental Congress. Jay was George Washington's secretary for Foreign Affairs, and in 1790 became the first chief justice of the Supreme Court.

John Jay

When the Declaration of Independence was being considered, John Jay was a moderate voice. He and John Dickinson got Congress to make one last try at getting along with the King of England—called the "Olive Branch" petition. In 1782, Jay and Benjamin Franklin went to Paris to help work out the terms of peace in the Treaty of Paris.

Jay was not at the Constitutional Convention, but he contributed to the *The Federalist Papers,* arguing for ratification of the new Constitution.

He was sent to England in 1784 to settle problems between the two countries. However, Jay's efforts were undercut by comments made by Alexander Hamilton. According to Hamilton, the United States wasn't going to make war on England in any case. The treaty that Jay agreed to turned out to be very unpopular in the states.

1777-78—The Best Men

When once an efficient national government is established, the best men in the country will not only consent to serve but also will be generally appointed to manage it.

Source: John Jay, in *The Federalist Papers,* found in Richard Hofstadter, William Miller, and Daniel Aaron, *The United States: History of a Republic,* Englewood Cliffs, New Jersey: Prentice-Hall, 1962, p 128.

Consider this:

Compare these lines to John Adams' prayer on page 11. Do you think that Jay's prediction has been true over the years?

Thomas Jefferson

Jefferson (1743–1826) was born in Virginia, where he inherited property from his father. After studying law, he became a member of the House of Burgesses (the colonial legislature). He became an early supporter of colonial rights, and his writings had a major influence on the colonists' decision to separate from England. Jefferson was a delegate to the Second Continental Congress, and the Declaration of Independence is almost completely his work.

In 1785, Jefferson was the minister to France, and he was there while the constitution was written and adopted. When he returned he became the nation's first secretary of state. He had many disagreements with the secretary of the treasury, Alexander Hamilton. Eventually, the two men led opposing political parties.

In the election of 1800, Jefferson and Aaron Burr tied for the presidency. The House of Representatives elected Jefferson, and Burr became vice president. Jefferson was the first President inaugurated in the new capitol, Washington, D.C.

He retired to Monticello in 1809, but still followed up his many interests, which included science and architecture. He believed in the importance of education, and one of his favorite projects was the development and founding of the University of Virginia. He died 50 years to the day after the formal Declaration of Independence—the same day that John Adams died.

Dates and Events—Thomas Jefferson

1760 Enters the College of William and Mary; after two years in college, studies law for five years

1767 Admitted to the bar

1769 Enters the House of Burgesses (the colonial legislature); becomes a leader among those who favor strong resistance to the British rulers

1774 Writes "A Summary View of the Rights of British America"

1775 Delegate to the Second Continental Congress

1776 Writes the Declaration of Independence

1772 Marries Martha Wayles Skelton; she dies in 1782, after the birth of their sixth child

1779 Elected governor of Virginia

1780-81 Writes "Notes on Virginia"

1782 Member of the Virginia delegation to the Continental Congress.

1784 Travels to France, joins Benjamin Franklin and John Adams in negotiating treaties; follows Franklin as U.S. minister to the French government

1790 Becomes George Washington's secretary of state

1797 Vice president under John Adams

1801-09 Becomes the third president, the first to be inaugurated in Washington, D.C.

1803 Makes the Louisiana Purchase

1809 Retires to Monticello

1825 Rector of the University of Virginia; Jefferson planned the university and designed its first buildings

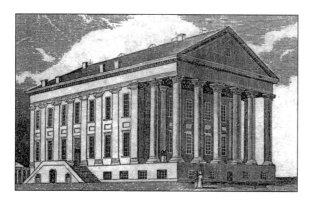

Thomas Jefferson also had a lot to do with how the new nation's official buildings looked. His design for the 1789 Virginia Capitol was based on a Roman Temple. See Discovery's Architecture: An Image for America.

In the Words of Thomas Jefferson

Summary:

We have expressed our complaints suitably for free people claiming their natural rights, not asking for gifts from their ruler. Let those who are afraid be flattering; that is not an American skill. It might be all right for the corrupt to give underserved praise, but it would seem wrong for those who speak for human rights. Such people know and say that Kings are the servants, not the owners of the people.

Commentary:

While the colonies still thought of themselves as "British America" Jefferson wrote a long document addressed to the king of England. These paragraphs come near the end.

Vocabulary:

derived = developed
grievance = cause for
    complaint
Magistrate = official; judge
sentiment = feeling
proprietor = owner
venal = one who can be
    bought; corrupt

1774—British-American Rights

… These are our grievances, which we have thus laid before his Majesty, with that freedom of language and sentiment which becomes a free people claiming their rights as derived from the laws of nature, and not as the gift of their Chief Magistrate. Let those flatter, who fear: it is not an American art. To give praise where it is not due might be well from the venal, but would ill [suit] those who are asserting the rights of human nature. They know, and will, therefore, say, that Kings are the servants, not the proprietors of the people.

The great principles of right and wrong are legible to every reader.... The whole art of government consists in the art of being honest.....

It is neither our wish nor our interest to separate from [Great Britain]....

Let them name their terms, but let them be just.... Let them not think to exclude us from going to other markets to dispose of those commodities which they cannot use, nor to supply those wants which they cannot supply. Still less, let it be proposed, that our properties, within our own territories, shall be taxed or regulated by any power on earth, but our own. The God who gave us life, gave us liberty at the same time: the hand of force may destroy, but cannot disjoin them.

Source: Thomas Jefferson, "A Summary View of the Rights of British America," *The Life and Selected Writings of Thomas Jefferson,* Adrienne Koch and William Peden, eds., New York: The Modern Library, 1972, pp. 293-311.

Summary:
Right and wrong are clear to every reader. The art of government is the art of being honest.

We do not want to separate from Great Britain, nor is that in our best interest.

Let them name their terms (for staying together), but let them be fair. They must not think of preventing us from selling goods they don't want in other markets. And our own property, in our own territory, should never be taxed or controlled by any other power on earth. The God who gave us life gave us liberty at the same time. Those things can be destroyed by force, but not separated.

Vocabulary:
commodities = items that are bought and sold
disjoin = separate; take apart
exclude = shut out; prevent something or someone from being included
legible = easy to read; easy to understand

Summary:

Our lively debates might have seemed odd to strangers not used to freely stating their thoughts. But the nation has decided according to the Constitution. Now everyone will accept the law and work together. Remember, though the will of the majority rules, the minority has equal rights and protection. It would be oppression to violate that. Let us work together with one heart and one mind.

Commentary:

In the 1800 presidential election, Thomas Jefferson and Aaron Burr each received 73 electoral votes. As the Constitution required, the House of Representatives met in a special session to choose the president. They debated and balloted for 30 hours. Finally, Jefferson was chosen president and Burr the vice president.

Vocabulary

animation = liveliness
aspect = appearance
exertion = great effort
prevail = prove stronger

1801—Jefferson's First Inaugural Address

During the contest of opinion through which we have passed the animation of discussions and of exertions has sometimes worn an aspect which might impose on strangers unused to think freely and to speak and to write what they think; but this being now decided by the voice of the nation, announced according to the rules of the Constitution, all will, of course, arrange themselves under the will of the law, and unite in common efforts for the common good. All, too, will bear in mind this sacred principle, that though the will of the majority is in all cases to prevail, that will to be rightful must be reasonable; that the minority possess their equal rights, which equal law must protect, and to violate would be oppression. Let us, then, fellow-citizens, unite with one heart and one mind.

Source: Thomas Jefferson, First Inaugural Address 1801, *Inaugural Addresses of the Presidents,* found at http://www.bartleby.com/124/pres16.html

James Madison

Madison (1751-1836) was born into a family of wealthy Virginia land-owners. He attended the College of New Jersey (now Princeton University), completing the four-year course in two years. During that time, he also joined in demonstrations against England and wrote poems making fun of members of a rival literary group.

As a member of the Virginia legislature, Madison wrote the Virginia Plan, which suggested a National Legislature with two branches, a National Executive (a president), and a National Judiciary. This plan was quite different from the government that had originally been set up under the Articles of Confederation.

Madison's notes provide our most complete record of the debates at the Constitutional Convention. After the document was adopted, he joined Hamilton and Jay in writing *The Federalist Papers.* Because of his efforts to develop the new Constitution and get it ratified, Madison is often called the Father of the Constitution.

He served in the House of Representatives and worked on the Bill of Rights. Madison soon found that he disagreed with Hamilton over the Bill of Rights and other matters. He became a member of the Republican party.

In 1797, Madison tried to retire from politics. But he was called on again and again for service and advice. Jefferson often relied on Madison, making him his secretary of state. In 1808, Madison was elected president.

Dates and Events—James Madison

1769	Enters the College of New Jersey (later Princeton University); completes the four-year course in two years
1774	Becomes an early voice for independence
1780	Delegate to the Continental Congress
1784	Member of the Virginia legislature
1787	Member of the Constitutional Convention
1777-78	Collaborates with Alexander Hamilton and John Jay on writing and publication of *The Federalist Papers*
1794	Marries Dolley Payne Todd
1797	Leaves Congress
1798	Drafts Virginia Resolutions in response to the Alien and Sedition Acts
1801-09	Secretary of state under Jefferson
1809	Elected fourth president of the United States;
1812	Reelected to presidency
1819	Helps Jefferson found the University of Virginia

In the Words of James Madison

Commentary:

As a member of the Virginia Legislature, Madison revealed problems with the government under the Articles of Confederation. Others agreed, and the final outcome was a new constitution.

Vocabulary:

conferred = given

determined = decided

inadequacies= flaws,
  weaknesses

proceeding = coming from

1786—Toward a New Government

Having witnessed ... the inadequacies of the powers conferred by the "Articles of Confederation" ... I felt it to be my duty to spare no efforts to impress on that body the alarming condition of the U. States proceeding from that cause, and the evils threatened by delay, in applying a remedy.... The convention proposed took place at Annapolis, in August, 1786.... [and that group] determined to recommend a convention, with enlarged powers, to be held the year following, in the city of Philadelphia.

Source: James Madison, letter to Thomas J. Wharton, August, 1827, "James Madison Tells the Story of the Constitutional Convention in His Letters," found at http.www.jmu.edu/maddescrdebates.htm

1787—Separate Branches

If it be a fundamental principle of free Govt [government], that the Legislative, Executive & Judiciary powers should be *separately* exercised, it is equally so that they be *independently* exercised.... A coalition of the [Executive and Legislative] powers would be more immediately & certainly dangerous to public liberty. It is essential then that the appointment of the Executive should either be drawn from some source, or held by some tenure that will give him a free agency with regard to the Legislature. This could not be if he was to be appointable from time to time by the legislature. ... The people at large was ... the fittest in itself. It would be as likely as any that could be devised to produce an Executive Magistrate of distinguished Character. The people generally could only know & vote for some Citizen whose merits had rendered him an object of general attention & esteem....

Source: James Madison, at the Constitutional Convention, July 20, 1787, found at http://www.jmu.edu/madison/quote.htm#founders

Summary:

If it is a basic rule of free government that the Legislative, Executive, and Judiciary powers should be separate, they must also be independent of each other. If the Executive and Legislative branches join together, that would put public freedom in danger. It is important that the Executive have freedom of action. He would not if he was appointed by the legislature. The people themselves are the best ones to choose him. That way is as likely as any to produce an excellent Executive. The people would only know and vote for someone who had already won their attention and high regard.

Vocabulary:

coalition = union
devised = thought of
Executive Magistrate =
   the president
   (Magistrate = official or
   judge)
exercised = carried out
free agency = freedom
   from responsibility to
   anyone else
rendered = made
tenure = length of service

Summary:

We had tiresome and repetitious discussions about whether the executive should be one person or a group of people working toward, how he should be appointed, how long he should hold office, whether he could run again.... Most members were satisfied with the solution we finally adopted.

Commentary:

Discussions at the Constitutional Convention weren't just over what a president did—but about what a president *was*. There had never been a president before.

Vocabulary:

co-ordinate = those who
   work together
duration = length of time
expedient = something
   done to achieve an aim
   quickly
mode = way of doing
   something
plurality = greater number
reiterated = repeated
   several times
subsequent = after
   something else

1787—Creating the Presidency

On the question whether [the presidency] should consist of a single person or a plurality of co-ordinate members, on the mode of appointment, on the duration in office, on the degree of power, on the re-eligibility, tedious and reiterated discussions took place.... The expedient at length adopted seemed to give pretty general satisfaction to the members....

It was much agitated whether a long term, seven years for example, with a subsequent and perpetual ineligibility, or a short term, with a capacity to be re-elected, should be fixed. In favor of the first opinion were urged the danger of … first a life and then hereditary tenure …

Summary:
It was hotly argued whether one long term of 7 years was best, or a short term with the possibility of reelection. Those in favor of one long term thought that reelection could lead to someone becoming president for life, or someone inheriting the office.

Vocabulary:
capacity = ability
hereditary = passed to
    the next generation
ineligibility =without legal
    status to hold office
perpetual = continuing
    for all time
subsequent = happening
    after something else
tenure = time in office

On the other side it was contended that the prospect of necessary degradation would discourage the most dignified characters from aspiring to the office; would take away the principal motive to the faithful discharge of its duties …

Source: James Madison, letter to Thomas Jefferson, October 24, 1787, "James Madison Tells the Story of the Constitutional Convention in His Letters," found at http.www.jmu.edu/maddescrdebates.htm

Summary:
The other side argued that the expectation of losing power would discourage our best for wanting the office, would take away the main reason for doing the job well.

Vocabulary:
contended = argued
degradation = loss of
    status; humiliation
discharge = carry out

George Mason (1725–92) was born in Virginia, where he became a well-to-do planter. He served in the Virginia House of Burgesses and was a member of the Constitutional Convention at Philadelphia in 1787.

George Mason

Mason wrote a Virginia declaration of rights, which Jefferson drew on when he wrote the Declaration of Independence. He also helped draft the Constitution. However, Mason had objections to the finished document. He didn't like the creation of such a strong central government, and he thought the Constitution should include a bill of rights. He refused to sign it.

Mason and Patrick Henry led the fight against Virginia's ratification of the Constitution. Many of Mason's suggestions were later included in the first 10 amendments (the Bill of Rights).

Consider this:
In what ways does the Declaration of Independence echo Mason's ideas?

Vocabulary:
fundamental = basic and necessary
maxim = rule; truth
consequently = as a result
derived from = obtained from

1775—Equality

We came equals into this world, and equals shall we go out of it. All men are by nature born equally free and independent. To protect the weaker from the injuries and insults of the stronger were societies first formed;… In all our associations; in all our agreements let us never lose sight of this fundamental maxim—that all power was originally lodged in, and consequently is derived from, the people.

Source: George Mason, in Robert Al Rutland, *The Papers of George Mason* (Chapel Hill, NC: University of North Carolina Press, 1970, 1:231, found at http://GunstonHall. org/georgemason/quotes.html

Gouverneur Morris, (1752-1816) was born in New York. He studied law, and helped draft the first state constitution. He was a member of the Continental Congress. He then moved to Philadelphia and took up his law practice there. In 1787, he was a member of the Constitutional Convention. From 1800-1803, he was a U.S. Senator from New York State.

Gouverneur Morris

During the Constitutional Convention, Morris was given the job of putting the new Constitution into the right words. In 1831, James Madison wrote in a letter that "The *finish* given to the style and arrangement of the Constitution fairly belong to the pen of Mr. Morris…." In order to avoid listing all the states by name, Morris began the document with the now famous line, "We the people of the United States…" Although Morris had some reservations about the finished product, he thought it was the best that could be worked out at the time. He urged Congress to accept it.

1811—Balanced Government

It was observed in the Convention at an early day … the necessity of drawing a line between national sovereignty and State independence … In the option between two evils, that which appeared to be the least was preferred, and the power of the union provided for. At present the influence of the general government has so thoroughly pervaded every State, that all the little wheels are obliged to turn according to the great one.

Source: Gouverneur Morris, letter to Robert Walsh, found on The Founder's Constitution website, http://press-pubs.uchicago.edu/founders

Summary:

We had to draw a line between national power and state independence. In the choice between two evils, we chose what seemed best. Now the central government forces every state to follow it.

Vocabulary:

pervaded = spread
  through
sovereignty = political
  independence

"The Landsdowne Portrait" of George Washington, by Gilbert Stuart, 1796

George Washington

Washington (1732-1799) was born in Virginia. He received only a few years of formal education, but learned enough math to take up the career of surveying. He had his first surveying job at age 16, and became an official county surveyor a year later.

At the age of 20, Washington was put in charge of training a county militia. In 1753, he volunteered to carry a message from Virginia's Governor Robert Dinwiddie to French troops that were moving into the Ohio territory —which he considered British property. That involved Washington in the French and Indian War, where he attracted attention by his bravery under fire.

When the first battles of the American Revolution began, John Adams suggested Washington for the command of the Continental army. Through the next long hard eight years, Washington held the ragged army together and held off the British. By the end of the war he was famous.

Washington wanted to retire to his home at Mount Vernon. But, like many others, he saw the weaknesses in the Articles of Confederation. He presided over the Constitutional Convention. Though he made few comments during the discussions, Washington's calm presence helped the members work out the new U.S. Constitution. When the time came to elect our first president, for many people Washington seemed to be the only possible choice.

Dates and Events—George Washington

1749   Holds first public office as surveyor

1752   Inherits Mount Vernon

1753   Put in charge of training a county militia

1754-55 Holds a military commission; in the French and Indian War he shows bravery under fire and gains rank of Colonel

1759   Marries Martha Custis; becomes a member of the Virginia House of Burgesses

1774   Delegate to the first Continental Congress; appointed Commander in Chief of army

1775-83 In command of the Continental army; fights the Revolutionary War

1783   Retires from the army, gives a farewell speech

1787   Presides over the Constitutional Convention in Philadelphia

1789   Unanimously elected president

1793   Reelected for a second term

1796   Refuses to run for a third term; retires from public life with a Farewell Address

In the Words of George Washington

1778—Celebrating the 4th

Tomorrow, the Anniversary of the Declaration of Independence will be celebrated by the firing thirteen Pieces of Cannon and …. The Soldiers are to adorn their Hats with *GreenBoughs* and to make the best appearance possible…. Double allowance of rum will be served out.

Source: George Washington, July 3, 1778, General Orders, in *The George Washington Papers at the Library of Congress,* found at http://memory.loc.gov/

Commentary:

The Continental army was always struggling with terrible circumstances. Still, Washington saw to it that they remembered what they were fighting for.

Summary:

Thinking about the complete achievement (sooner than should have been expected) of the goal for which we fought—against so great a power—must fill us with amazement and gratitude. The disadvantages we were under can never be forgotten. The unequalled determination of the army, through every possible suffering and discouragement for 8 long years, was little short of a miracle.

Commentary:

It had been a long and terrible war. Washington's farewell to his troops was an emotional occasion.

Vocabulary:

attainment = achievement of a goal

compleat = complete

contemplation = thinking about

disadvantageous = not helpful

formidable = difficult; causing dread

perseverence = persistence in spite of difficulties

unparalleled = unequalled

1783—Farewell to the Band of Brothers

A contemplation of the compleat attainment (at a period earlier than could have been expected) of the object for which we contended against so formidable a power cannot but inspire us with astonishment and gratitude. The disadvantageous circumstances on our part, under which the war was undertaken, can never be forgotten. The… unparalleled perseverence of the Armies of the U States, through almost every possible suffering and discouragement for the space of eight long years, was little short of a standing miracle.

A detail from George Washington at the Battle of Princeton, NJ, 1777. (Courtesy of The Mount Vernon Ladies' Association)

It is not the meaning nor within the compass of this address to detail the hardships peculiarly incident to our service, or to describe the distresses, which in several instances have resulted from the extremes of hunger and nakedness, combined with the rigours of an inclement season; nor is it necessary to dwell on the dark side of our past affairs. Every American Officer and Soldier must now [remember] the uncommon scenes in which he has been called to Act no inglorious part, and the astonishing events of which he has been a witness, events which have seldom if ever before taken place on the stage of human action, nor can they probably ever happen again. For who has before seen a disciplined Army form'd at once from such raw materials? Who, that was not a witness, could imagine that the most violent local prejudices would cease so soon, and that Men who came from the different parts of the Continent, strongly disposed, by the habits of education, to despise and quarrel with each other, would instantly become but one patriotic band of Brothers … ?

Source: George Washington to the Continental Army, November 2, 1783, Farewell Orders, in *The George Washington Papers at the Library of Congress,* found at http://memory.loc.gov/

Summary:

It is not my intention to describe our hardships or distress. Sometimes they resulted from hunger and nakedness, combined with the terrible winters. It is not necessary to dwell on the dark side of our past. Every American officer and soldier must remember the rare events in which he participated, and the amazing events he saw. Such events have seldom if ever before taken place in human life, and probably will never happen again. For who ever saw a disciplined Army formed so fast from such inexperienced recruits? Who, without seeing it, could imagine that the strongest prejudices would disappear so fast? That men from different places, taught to hate and quarrel with each other, would instantly became one patriotic band of Brothers?

Vocabulary:
compass = range; scope
disposed = likely
inclement = stormy, rainy, or snowy weather
inglorious = unrecognized
rigours = rigor; hardship

45

Summary:

Among life's surprises, nothing could have given me greater concern than your message. I was called by my country, which I respect and love. But the size and difficulty of the job to which my country called me was enough to make anyone question his suitability. For someone born with inferior talents and lacking management experience, it must cause despair. Such a person ought to be especially aware of his own shortcomings. I only hope that, in taking this job, if I have been too much swayed by your confidence, my error will seem less serious because of my reasons.

Vocabulary:

dispondence = being despondent; unhappy
endowments = natural abilities
incident = accompanying
magnitude = great size
qualification = what makes one suitable for a job
scrutiny = careful study
palliated = made to seem less serious
veneration = reverence
vicissitudes = unexpected changes

1789—The First Presidential Inaugural Address

Fellow Citizens of the Senate and the House of Representatives.

Among the vicissitudes incident to life, no event could have filled me with greater anxieties than [your notification of my election]…. On the one hand, I was summoned by my Country, whose voice I can never hear but with veneration and love…. On the other hand, the magnitude and difficulty of the trust to which the voice of my Country called me, being sufficient to awaken in the wisest and most experienced of her citizens, a distrustful scrutiny into his qualification, could not but overwhelm with dispondence, one, who, inheriting inferior endowments from nature and unpractised in the duties of civil admini'stration, ought to be peculiarly conscious of his own deficencies…. All I dare hope, is, that if in executing this task I have been too much swayed by … the confidence of my fellow citizens … my error will be palliated by the motives which misled me …

Source: George Washington to Congress, April 30, 1789, First Inagural Address, in *The George Washington Papers at the Library of Congress,* found at http://memory.loc.gov

Afterword: Heroes

by Pat Perrin

Many of our nation's founders were aware of something heroic about what they and others were doing. They knew that the government they were creating was different from anything yet invented. They even realized that they were becoming famous.

At that time, people thought about fame a little differently than now. Virtue (moral goodness) and fame were believed to be connected. Public acclaim had to be earned through honesty, honor, and courage. James Wilson, a friend and ally of James Madison, taught his law students that we are born with a natural desire for fame and honor. Wilson said that "The love of reputation and the fear of dishonor are, by the all-gracious Author of our existence, implanted in our breasts, for purposes the most beneficent and wise." (Source: Quoted in Garry Wills, *Cincinnatus: George Washington & the Enlightenment,* New York: Doubleday, 1984, p 129)

Our founders were famous men even in their own time. Benjamin Franklin was so highly thought of that an artist named Charles Willson Peale "hoped, with his taxidermist's skills, to preserve Franklin's body for display in his museum." (Source: Garry Wills, *Cincinnatus,* p. 196)

According to Wills (p. 197), by 1788, Pennsylvanians were singing:

> Great Washington shall rule the land,
> While Franklin's counsel guides his hand.

What Will History Say?

The history of our Revolution will be … that Dr. Franklin's electric rod smoth the earth and out sprung General Washington. That Franklin electrised him with his rod, and thence-forward these two conducted all the policy, negotiations, legislatures, and war.

Source: John Adams, 1790 letter to Benjamin Rush, quoted in Garry Wills, *Cincinnatus: George Washington & the Enlightenment,* New York: Doubleday, 1984, p. 197.

Commentary:

Sometimes we seem to believe that our greatest heroes miraculously accomplished everything all by themselves. John Adams realized that some Revolutionary leaders were already being turned into bigger-than-life characters.

One problem with having heroes is that they never seem quite human. Sometimes it's hard to remember that the founders of our nation all had their faults and weaknesses. They often disagreed with each other. The more you read about them, the more you'll probably begin to recognize their everyday humanity—and the ways in which they rose above it.

Charles Francis Adams was the the son of John Quincy Adams. In 1841, he considered the nature of heroes when he wrote a memoir for a collection of the letters of Abigail Adams.

Summary:
Our history is about those who hold office. Great Revolutionary leaders seem like heroes of mythology. They're seen on stage, where they must hide or sacrifice their true feelings for the good of all. Politicians and generals seldom say what they really think or feel. The result is that, in their writing, they appear very serious. Though that doubtless impresses later generations, it makes them seem uninteresting.

Consider this:
What image does the line "made to assume a uniform of grave hue" give you of these heroes?

Vocabulary:
consequence = result
exalts = raises
posterity = future
   generations
sentiment = feeling

The words of Charles Francis Adams— "Like Heroes of a Mythological Age"

Our history is for the most part wrapped up in the forms of office. The great men of the Revolution, in the eyes of posterity, are, many of them, like heroes of a mythological age. They are seen, for the most part, when conscious that they are acting upon a theatre, where individual sentiment must be sometimes disguised, and often sacrificed, for the public good. Statesmen and generals rarely say all they think or feel. The consequence is, that, in the papers which come from them, they are made to assume a uniform of grave hue, which, though it doubt-less exalts the opinion later generations may entertain of their perfections, somewhat diminishes the interest with which they study their character. …

Source: Charles Francis Adams, "Memoir," in Letters of Mrs. Adams, the Wife of John Adams, Boston: Charles C Little and James Brown, 1841, pp. xvii-xix.

In his memoir, Charles Francis Adams goes on to say that these famous men were influenced by their fellow-citizens. They were expressing a moral principle that was shared by others. "Their strength against Great Britain was not that of numbers, nor of wealth, nor of genius; but it drew its nourishment from the sentiment that pervaded the dwellings of the entire population."

In that population, Charles Francis Adams included women.

The Influence that Escapes Observation

How much this home sentiment did then, and does ever, depend upon the character of the female portion of the people, will be too readily understood by all, to require explanation. The domestic hearth is the first of schools, and the best of lecture-rooms … And this is the scene for the almost exclusive sway of the weaker sex. Yet, great as the influence thus exercised undoubtedly is, it escapes observation in such a manner, that history rarely takes much account of it.

Source: Charles Francis Adams, "Memoir," in Letters of Mrs. Adams, the Wife of John Adams, Boston: Charles C Little and James Brown, 1841, pp. xvii-xix.

Summary:
How much this depends on women is too obvious to need explaining. Home is the first school and the best lecture room. And it is completely influenced by women. No matter how great this influence, it's rarely noticed.

Vocabulary:
domestic = home; family
exclusive = limited to one group
exercised = carried out
sway = influence

Charles Francis Adams was clearly aware that his grandmother, Abigail Adams had a part in the creation of our nation. Although women could not hold power during her lifetime—or for many years afterward—the letters Abigail Adams exchanged with her husband show her understanding of the events that swirled around her.

We'll end with her words, on the following page.

Abigail Adams (1744-1818) is the woman most often listed among those who created our nation. Born in Massachusetts, she was the wife of the second president and the mother of the sixth. She and her husband were often separated by his political activities, but they wrote to each other constantly. John Adams always addressed her as his "Dearest Friend."

In the Words of Abigail Adams

Commentary:

Like many of the founders, Abigail Adams was convinced that the colonies would soon separate from England and write their own laws. Like few of the male founders, she saw that women must become a part of the political process. Mostly self-educated, she always regretted that the education of women was so neglected.

Vocabulary:

foment = stir up
philosophers = those who
   studied basic ideas
tyrants = absolute and
   unjust rulers

1776—Revolutionary Advice

I long to hear that you have declared an independancy—and by the way in the new Code of Laws which I suppose it will be necessary for you to make I desire you would Remember the Ladies, and be more generous and favor-able to them than your ancestors. Do not put such unlimited power into the hands of the Husbands. Remember all men would be tyrants if they could. If particular care and attention is not paid to the Laidies we are determined to foment a Rebelion, and will not hold ourselves bound by any Laws in which we have no voice, or Representation.

Source: Abigail Adams, letter to her husband, March 31, 1776. In *The Columbia World of Quotations,* 1996, found at http:www.bart1eby.com

If we mean to have heroes, statesmen, and phi-losophers, we should have learned women.

Source: Abigail Adams, letter to her husband, August 14, 1776. In *The Columbia World of Quotations,* 1996, found at http:www.bart1eby.com

Research Activities/Things to Do

Thoughts on Term Limits - Still an issue today!

James Madison

"No man can be a competent legislator who does not add to an upright intention and a sound judgement a certain degree of knowledge of the subjects on which he is to legislate. A part of this knowledge may be acquired by means of information which lie within the compass of men in private as well as public stations. Another part can only be attained, or at least thoroughly attained, by actual experience in the station which requires the use of it.... A few of the members [of Congress], as happens in all such assemblies, will possess superior talents; will, by frequent re-elections, become members of long standing; will be thoroughly masters of the public business, and perhaps not unwilling to avail themselves of those advantages. The greater the proportion of new members and the less the information of the bulk of the members, the more apt will they be to fall into the snares that may be laid for them." (The Federalist, #53)

Samuel Adams

"If ever time should come, when vain and aspiring men shall possess the highest seats in Government, our country will stand in need of its experienced patriots to prevent its ruin." (1780)

"Much safer is it, and much more does it tend to promote the welfare and happiness of society to fill up the offices of Government after the mode prescribed in the American Constitution, by frequent elections of the people. They may indeed be deceived in their choice; they sometimes are; but the evil is not incurable; the remedy is always near; they will feel their mistakes, and correct them." (1790)

Roger Sherman

"Frequent elections are necessary to preserve the good behavior of rulers. They also tend to give permanency to the Government, by preserving that good behavior, because it ensures their re-election.... In Connecticut we have existed 132 years under an annual government; and as long as a man behaves himself well, he is never turned out of office." (From Madison's notes at the Constitutional Convention, 1787)

Source: *The Founding Fathers on Term Limits*, Vol. 12, No. 12, June 10, 1996.

- Evaluate the excerpts above using the written document form on the page 52. Then compare the three views on term limits to each other and to the term limits issue of today.

Written Document Worksheet

1. **Type of document:**

   ❑ Newspaper   ❑ Diary/Journal   ❑ Letter

   ❑ Ad   ❑ Telegram   ❑ Patent

   ❑ Deed   ❑ Census Report   ❑ Memo

   ❑ Report   ❑ Other _____

2. **Clues about the Document:**

   ❑ Interesting Stationery   ❑ "RECEIVED"

   ❑ Fold Marks   ❑ "CLASSIFIED"

   ❑ Handwritten   ❑ Written Notations

   ❑ Typed   ❑ "TOP SECRET" Stamp

   ❑ "Copy"   ❑ Official

3. **Date(s) of Document:**   ❑ No Date

4. **Author of Document:**   **Position:**

5. **For what audience was the document written?**

6. **Key information** *(What do you think are the three most important points?)*

   1.

   2.

   3.

7. **Choose a quote from the document that helped you to know why it was written.**

8. **Write down two clues which you got from the document that tell you something about life in the U.S. at the time it was written.**

   1.

   2.

9. **Write a question to the author that you feel is unanswered in the document.**